THOUGHT CATALOG BOOKS

No One Reads Poetry

No One Reads Poetry

A Collection of Poems

ABBY ROSMARIN

Thought Catalog Books

Brooklyn, NY

THOUGHT CATALOG BOOKS

Copyright © 2016 by Abby Rosmarin.

All rights reserved. Published by Thought Catalog Books, a division of The Thought & Expression Co., Williamsburg, Brooklyn. Founded in 2010, Thought Catalog is a website and imprint dedicated to your ideas and stories. We publish fiction and non-fiction from emerging and established writers across all genres. For general information and submissions: manuscripts@thoughtcatalog.com.

First edition, 2016

ISBN 978-0692721018

10 9 8 7 6 5 4 3 2 1

Cover photography by © Abby Rosmarin

For all of the muses in my life.

And for a universe that insists on getting its way on everything.

Contents

Daylight

I'm losing daylight on
this precious life

I have no more time to stay
stuck inside

After You're Done Being a Doormat

Just like any real doormat, once you're done
being used, you must
pick yourself up
by the corners and
shake the dust off – perhaps
a more drastic shakeup, or a violent
whip-crack in the air
for any remaining dirt, letting
what was once on you be introduced back
to the world

And then, like any doormat, you have a choice
whether you go back down by the door, down
as the welcome mat, pretending
you are in control, because you decided
whether you were placed on
the inside or out, or you go
someplace else, find a new spot
far from the boots and sandals and dirty feet

3

Insanity

Let's reveal and
revel and rebel in our insanity, instead of
slathering on another coat of paint
as the veneer cracks
along the sides

The Day Before My Father Passed

I call to check in
and get the answering machine

The message greeting me
is now automated, already replacing
my father's voice, the one that
greeted all callers since I was a child

Not his voice, not my mom's,
but a robot tells me to
leave a message

At the tone I forget what I was going to say.

Problems

Some mornings I wake up before my
problems do, and I can
take a shower in peace

I can prepare my coffee and
collect my things without
collecting my thoughts
I can get ready for the day with
easy breath and I can pretend
every morning feels like this.

But it does not take long before the problems awake
before they stretch and yawn and open their eyes
taking a few cautious steps out of bed before walloping me
upside the head
reminding me as they follow behind
exactly where I am

The Holidays

"How weird," I said as we
drive around, "People
right now are spending today
with their families."

"So are you," he says from
the driver's seat, slipping his hand
into mine.

A Misconception of Pain

Pain
is not weakness
leaving the body

Pain
is the body attempting
to be stronger
than its environment

Trial by Fire

This trial by fire has burned away
everything
that wasn't me, every
façade and clinging dream, every
false hope, or
toxicity – every
single thing, until
all that was left was
who I was always supposed to be, with
ashes and soot and
smoldering cinders
surrounding my feet

9

Home

The house is so silent sometimes that I
stomp up and down stairs
turning on music and clanking away the
odds and ends

So silent that I need to step outside and
hear the rustle of the wind
the crunch of the leaves
and the reminder that the walls won't close
in on me
when I go back in

10

Minimize

"You minimize," he says.
"You do everything you can
to avoid conflict."

And all I can do
is sit there
wondering what I can say
to make this stop.

Construction

This whole town is under construction.

The roads are dug up, and
concrete pipes lay by its side
The manholes are raised, cones and signs
and backhoes and dump trucks and
police officers line the streets.

"It's ugly now, but
it will look so nice, when it's all done,"
I tell myself.

This upkeep,
I tell myself,
is a vital part of life.

You have to dig up and destroy before
you can create and improve.

Traffic is at a standstill, the officer
directing us around
a giant ditch,
cones around the edge, the front end loader
digging away.

I watch the lights go green, go red,
go green again.

"I should be moving,"
I tell myself,
I can't be still, can't be stuck
can't handle being in the midst of this
reconstruction.

What wouldn't I give for a detour around
to a multi-lane highway, circumventing the whole mess
the demolishing and the reconstructing

The wind in my hair instead
and old, well-worn roads before me

and my foot predictably off
the brake pedal.

Broken

And once I said, "I'm tired
of going around, pretending
like we're not all broken
in some way," – the rest of the world seemed
to open up for me.

Gentle Envy

Oh the gentle envy I feel
for every person he meets, every
person he interacts with, talks to, hugs,
every person he has on the phone
or on the line

The gentle envy
for people I might not know, people
who some exist only in theory, or
whose lives I might never want, but a desire, still
to be them, just for that time, that
five minutes, that hour, that temporary span

To live a life of jumping
from person to person, in their skin
for the length he interacts with them, then moving on
to the next – in my skin only
when it's my turn

All this just to have
one more word, one more
hug, one more set of
connections
Another addition to the insatiable need
for his voice, his touch, his time and energy

14

Projection

She viewed the world
like a canvas, a blank sheet, something
flat and white to take in
what she projected out: her
ideas and ideals, what she thought
the world should be and how it all
should go

And how angry she got
whenever she found paint
and texture, scenes already drawn out

landscapes and portraits interrupting
her perfected projection

Observations in Ohio

Last year:
A middle school in this
small town
attached a banner to the front
of their building,

a sign, proudly
proclaiming they had scored
"adequate"
on some type of
public school review.

This year:
"For Sale: Former School"
sits in front of the building instead.

Destruction in the Distance

I crawl back to bed one
last time
cuddling into him like my morning coffee
cradled in his arms like I'd cradle my mug

my face to his shirt, taking in the aroma
of old cotton and sleeping sweat
like fresh grounds, freshly brewed

I stay to the last minute, joking
that I'll fall back asleep if I stay any more
and remove myself
from the room

I drive into the dawn, the sun
gently rising through
the cold air around me

the morning mist and the orange sky
make the world look like it's on fire, like there's
destruction in the distance, and smoke blinding the way.

For the Departed

If I believe, truly
believe
our souls
are meant to cross paths, in each and
every life, traversing millennia and
repeating
this sweet interaction time and
time again

Then what is one lifetime
where those interactions are
cut short

Future

And with a frenzied,
frightened,
anxious heart,

she tumbled
headfirst
into the life she was destined to live.

Don't Tell Me

Don't tell me listen to my heart, like
it's an advice line I can dial in – when
my heart has done nothing but send me down
backroads and alleys and
gritty neighborhoods
only to backtrack and retrace and
end up at square one and
turning to me for direction

Don't tell me to listen to my heart
when it isn't the same one from yesterday
when one version will give an answer only
to contradict
and evolve

Don't tell me to listen to my heart
when it has matchsticks and gasoline
when it's ready to set fire
and destroy whatever it is it sees

Don't tell me
to listen to my heart
when I'm busy talking it down from its ledge

20

Shoelaces

He ties my shoes too tight, to keep my shoe
in place
from front to base, he tugs each loop taught
until I swear the lace will break

"It hurts," I say.

"It's for the best," he says.

"Trust me.
This is what you need."

But it's not.

My feet spent the entire time
in pain, the only good that came
are the callouses

for the next time
he pulls the laces too tight

A Sign

"Confirmation bias," I tell
myself, "And
selective attention.
Coincidence and chance and
nothing special."

I say to
myself as I take it in
like a clear-cut, deliberate
message
from a higher power

The Real To Do

Nowhere
on my
to-do list
does
it
say
to throw myself
a pity party

So it's time to get up
and take my list
and get something done
before the clown and balloons arrive

Substitute

If there is a stronger word
than "miss",
to substitute in
the phrase:

"I miss you."

Let me know.

And I'll make sure
to use that
instead
when talking about you.

Feral

And as I heard him say those words, as
the rumbles and grumbles had
turned to growls

That's when I knew
that this lion-hearted man
had gone feral

Mutual Crazies

I desire nothing more than to see
what rests beneath, what moves and shakes
within you, for I know they would be the
perfect dance partners
for what's underneath my own

We are all dinged and dented
and scratched
We are all made of crazy glue residue from
trying to piece the shards together

I have no interest in the polished façade
or pretending your presence makes
my damage disappear

I want nothing more than to reveal our mutual stories
and what swims beneath the surface, so
I can prove what I already know: that your
dings and dents and shards and breaks
line up well with my own

One More

One more crying fit, one more
set of tears, before
I dry my eyes, splash
water on my face
and walk through the door like
nothing has happened

In Memoriam

The place looks nothing like it was before

They've moved out the furniture and
repainted the walls
Gone are the knick-knacks, decorations, comforts
Gone are the coat racks and coats, seats and tables
Curtains and cabinets and lampshades

Gone is every single thing from that time
but the burning memory of what once was

and no amount of paint can scrub that from the walls

28

Simple Act

To hold hands
simply
holding hands, while
getting irretrievably lost
in conversation, in
each other's eyes
– anchored down by nothing more
than the simple feel
of palms pressed together
and
fingers resting between
the other's knuckles

The most intimate sweet
nothingness
that the poets
and the playwrights of the world
could only hope to recreate

Rest

As you go about your day, your
busy and exhausting and stressful day, darting
from one appointment to the next, know that
a part of you always rests
in the ramshackle shelter of my heart

Meaning

Let me search for meaning
under
desk chairs and shelves
in closets and behind doors

Let me desperately search
for meaning, in every
single
thing
I do or see

Searching, like a private eye,
my camera
and notebook close at hand, ready
to capture meaning as it
sneaks out of vehicles
or into apartments

Desperately searching
for meaning
in everything
by any means
like it'll culminate in reward
if found and
returned

Let me find meaning
like payday hinges on its capture

Life is What Happened

Life is what happened
during those times
you kept yourself busy
trying not
to think about him

Decorations

Because I have no interest in
decorating
I will pull out the box of seasonal goods

Because it's the last thing I want
to do
I will put out knick knacks
and themed items
and
make everything festive

Because all I want to do is
curl into a corner and cry
I will decorate that corner
with glitter and gold
and garland and cheer

33

Nostalgic

I'm waiting for the day
when these songs don't transport me

When these notes don't act
like chauffeurs, driving me
directly to a bubbled-in
place, preserved and frozen
in time

When the chorus and the bridge and the opening lines
don't direct me back
to a place so dark and secluded and
tragic and beautiful, a place
encapsulated in that bubble
and preserved and frozen in time

I'm waiting for the day
when the melody doesn't speed away
leaving me stranded
in the world of what once had been

Insufferable

There's a supreme
sadness
about her
And I try to focus on that
as she continues
to grind my gears

Who You Are

Please do not change who you are.

Please do not look at these men – these lovers
who take in what they can when it benefits them and
walk away when it stops – and decide
that it means you are unlovable.

Please do not mistake that fire in your heart for a burning in a
building,

something that needs to set off the alarms and the sprinkler
systems
and be put out.
Please do not think for a second that a careless heart is some-
how an indictment on you.

Please do not change who you are.

You are the poetry that reveals the beauty in the tragedy.
You are the enthusiasm in the most mundane.
You bring a passion to the everyday and God help anyone
who mistakes that
for insanity.

You are all that you are,
good and bad

up and down
negative and positive. You are human,
capable of the whole scope of experiences and tastes and
explanations.
Do not feel that you have to subdue all that you are because of
the hurricane that resides with the rest of your weather.

Be that hurricane!

Let them choose the easier girls.
They are after the McDonalds, easy and convenient
and unsatisfying.

They'll learn.

They will learn even the easy girls have nuance.
They will learn that the easy girls are not even girls in the first
place,
but women.
Women with a juvenile label and a crafted demeanor they
hope
comes off as low maintenance.
They'll learn even the easy ones are difficult, with their wants
and desires
and opinions

and they'll move on once again.

Because there is no easy in love. There is no easy in being
human.

It is not love to go after the girl who simply

giggles at jokes and admires silently and
acquiesces instantly – all in the name of said

low maintenance.

It is not love to sidle up to the equivalent of a live studio audi-
ence,
laughing and applauding on cue and staying
silent otherwise.

It is not love to be with someone who never shows
the side of themselves that is not always the calm serene
spring.

It is selfish and careless companionship and it is destined to
be doomed.

Embrace your storm!

You will find nothing to gain by berating yourself.
There is no prize, no metal,
no achievement in telling yourself that it is wrong to be sad,
to be angry
or envious
or insecure.
There is nothing awaiting you if you decide to drop your pur-
suits and desires in the name of
"cute".
You are all of that, the same way every one us of is all of that.
If a lover steps away, embrace that it just wasn't meant to be.

Embrace that new storm and move on.

Be open
to love, to communication, to
the feelings and emotions of another human being.

The rest are details

to be fulfilled and complemented when the right one comes
along.

And he will come along.

Let his storm feed your storm,

not in a way that enhances destruction
but
in a way that brings out both's natural power.

You are exactly what someone is looking for, somewhere.

So please, do not change who you are.

Task At Hand

What am I going to do
when the chores are done and the
appointments made, when every
task is finished and every
assignment complete

What am I going to do when
I reach the end of my busy-ness
and am left with nothing but the things
I have to face

At Some Point

At some point
the traffic will ease and
you will move on.

At some point
the season will end and
deadlines will pass and
this, too, as well.

At some point
the pain will ease – and
you will move on.

Definitions

Amor
(Spanish, verb)
to love

Armor
(English, noun)
a hard, protective
covering
designed to
keep things out, to
avoid the consequences of
being vulnerable

Fascinating,
the overlaps
between languages and
definitions

Dead Ends

My my
this must be
the most beautiful
dead end road I've ever had
the pleasure
of barreling headfirst down

Companion

Darling you are with me

You are with me everywhere I go.

You are with me when I fall asleep and when I wake up.

You are with me in my dreams and
in my daydreams. You are with me
in every sunrise, every sunset, every touch,
every caress.

You are with me when I smile and
you are with me when my heart aches.
You are with every fluctuation of the day.

You are with me when I
greet the day and you are with me when I
go another day
without you.

You are with me even
when I swear it would be easier
to go at this alone

You are with me
truly, as I can only hope

in ways that I am also
with you

41

The Truth About Poetry

Let's get one thing straight:
poetry is selfish.

Poetry is saying,
"My words are beyond prose, beyond reproach
and beyond the rules of syntax and structure."

It is self-involved to describe your heart
in sing-song and free verse and
iambic beat

It is self-obsessed to look and say,
"Someone will resonate with this."

Poetry is saying, "This experience needs to be
written in
such
a
specific
way.
And I'll follow the rules, or
make them up as I go."

And the foolish thing
the foolhardy thing, is that
we believe this.

We write and we send it out, pretending like this
is a selfless act
and hoping
someone else
agrees.

Samskaras

Breathe in anxiety and
breathe out love
Be aware and
self-aware

Understand motivations and follow
innovation
Cut ties with the toxic and
pursue what makes you grow

Avoid hazards, avoid patterns
avoid falling into traps
Breathe in worry and
breathe out empathy

This cycle ends with me.

85

43

Stories

Tell me your stories

Start with the adventures, the
misadventures, then move on to what
makes you tick

Tell me the comedies, the
tragedies, the triumphs and mistakes
Your childhood, your
traumas, your hang-ups and
quirks. Tell me about
anything, everything – tell me
your annotated and expurgated
and completely tangled history

Then tell me more

Weave the stories together, weave together
the past and the present, the good and
the bad, the light and the dark, angels and
demons – sew together
the patchwork I am desperate for

Then I'll show you
exactly where

the stitches overlap
with my own

Sodden

Darling
if you only knew

The universe is sodden
with the words I want to say to you

45

Productivity

There are so many things
so many
better
more productive uses
of my time

Then to stare at this screen
mindlessly scrolling
waiting
for this feeling to pass.

Juxtapositions

A detention center rests at the base of
one of the prettiest views in town.

A cruel juxtaposition if you ask me —but then again,
what is life but a set of cruel juxtapositions

Shackles and vistas, beauty and pain
the worst at the base of the best
Prisons of our own creating and false sense of freedom

47

Highway Etiquette

Driving on the highway requires
checking your blind spots, your
rear view mirror, your speed

Keeping an eye out for
swerving cars and
speed traps, making sure
you're on the right route, that
you're in the right lane, that
you didn't miss your exit

Certainly
there are too many things to do.
There is no room on the highway
to be engulfed in tears, to the point
that the radio's music is drowned out and
you forget where you are

Take Warning

The morning sky's a rippled wave of red,
stretching out until
the whole world is bathed in rouge

This red sky at morning
I can't think
of a lovelier way
to warn the world that a storm's approaching

Normal Life

Wake up the next morning.

Tend to your pets, your
garden, take in the morning air

Brush, shower, get ready
for your day, go through your routines, your
rituals
And talk with a smile on your face

Breathe in, breathe out,
return an email, an office call
Check something off your to-do list and make
dinner plans for tomorrow

Go about your life
pretending
that everything has not irrevocably changed

In Response

And all
I could do
was sit there
and love him with
every ounce of my soul

The Heart is a Heavy Thing

The heart is a heavy thing, pulling
down and back in the chest, drumming out
its rhythmic dance, or weighted so much
the lung strain to stay in place
So heavy it can pull the shoulders down, sink feet into the
floor
Make the soul feel pressed, as if
it will never get up

The heart is a heavy thing, weighing
down deep and back against the chest

20/20 Foresight

My eyesight is good, but even I
can't look past
the immediate situation and clearly
see
the bigger plan at hand

Revert

Strength is a fragile, fluid concept

I'm always one
misstep, one
snide remark, one
measly mile

away

from complete
self doubt and total
exhaustion

And a rogue thought away
from bursting into tears

Breadcrumbs

As I walk, I hope to
drop my sorrow behind me along
the way
like breadcrumbs to a trail
I hope to never trace back

Questions

You make me ask all sorts of questions
– questions like, "Did we meet in a previous life?"
"How was your day?"
"When will I see you next? Will I see you again?"
"Who could have predicted this?"

And

"How am I supposed to move on – how can I take
even a single step
away from something like this?"

Self Destruction

I think
I'm so keen

On tearing these walls and
setting fire
to what's around me

Because I'm done with life being
built around me
instead of me
building life for myself

New Roads

I know I need to drive down new roads
as I attempt to process all that's
going on

Because all the old thoughts and sensations
await me on the familiar, repeated streets
hanging out by curves and bends I know by heart
hiding by trees I've passed by and
jumping out at red lights
making its presence felt in tired routes
cementing exactly what I need to let go

So I will drive down this street with the windows down
and my arms out the window, my
fingers dancing through the air
caressing the wind, taking in the world
around me like a lost and cherished friend
getting desperately lost as I try
to be desperately found

Waste of Time

Perhaps what we want
will never be
in the cards
for us

But darling

I will never consider this
a waste of my time.

After Effects

The flowers wilted long ago.
The ones that hadn't been disposed of
grew soggy at the stem
sitting in old water

The cards have been opened and read
and the baked goods have all
been eaten

The phone calls all answered and returned, thank yous
given
The comfort food you
bought yourself now
itself a memory

All that remains are the after effects:
clean the vase, file away the cards,
sweep the floor of crumbs, plan
your next diet
As you digest what has happened, as you let the reality of
mourning
settle

Telephone

A father
who never called
on Christmas
on birthdays
to say hello
to check in

calls other family members
to complain
that his daughter doesn't call enough

The Laundry

I fold the week's laundry, pacing
the floor as I do, reciting out the week's things
I did not say
to the air around me

Telling a sweatshirt how
unfair it has been
and reprimanding a pair of pants for what they said
And bemoaning my fears to the stack of towels
admitting to the t-shirt that I miss it
while telling the rolled up socks to leave

I call the dish cloth out, listing my grievances
as one stacks one top of the other
until I've at last sorted out everything
that I needed sorting out

62

Motivated

He makes me want
to write poetry, he makes me
want to write love letters
every single
day.

He makes me want
to be nothing more
than me, all of me, the version of me
that hits the borders and fills the brims
of my deepest potential

He makes me want
– and it makes me learn to live
with wanting, learning to be
stronger
than the want
because he makes me want
to be as a strong
as I could ever be.

63

Two Vastly Different Scenes

Corner in the city, a man
speaks animatedly to a
woman on the curb, his
hand and gestures wild, her
face scrunched up – another
off to the side, nonresponsive

and I surreptitiously stare

trying to see
if she's laughing or crying
if she's amused or
fighting tears

the fine line in body language
between two vastly different
scenes

Venus

Like a misguided North Star
Venus shines bright
in the new day's sky

...And like a traveler
hellbent
on getting lost
I follow it South by Southeast

Prodigal Daughter

These days,

church

is like an odd homecoming, the
prodigal daughter half-heartedly returns.

A decade later, after
an evolution of belief: devout to doubt
atheist, agnostic – questioning and questing before
eventually slipping into my own
definition of God, the way
one slips into a hand-knit sweater

church

these days

feels like an old pair of shoes, now
one size too small.

66

Why I'm Here

I do not sit here because you're cute.

I do not stay because of your wit
and charm, your
creative heart or
indomitable drive

I'm not here because you
can make me laugh, or that face you make
when impersonating others, the way
you cock an eyebrow and
contort your mouth

Or the way your shoulders drop
at a heavy thought, or the simple joy of
resting my head in that space

I do not stay because you're
easy on the eyes, or easy to talk to

I sit here because you're
easy on the soul – a soul I swear
resides as much in you as it does in me

Not because my heart flutters or
pleads

but because the spirit goes, "Yes.
Yes.
This.
All of this.
This is what they meant, what
transcends the linear and the logic."

Because the simple joy of
simply being here in this same space
rests deep in the bones, still there, even
when the surface level
and ease of it all
is taken away

Because the soul says yes
I stay.

Zombified

Feelings buried alive
will only dig themselves up
out of the grave

with more malice
than before

68

Harbinger

How beautiful the dusk sun is

until I realize how early
I'm seeing it.

The days are getting shorter. This
warmth will soon be gone
and I sigh at the dynamic, how something
so nice and be a harbinger for something
so dark.

69

Like No One's Watching

Early morning, the first awake,
headphones already in, with
music that hits a little too hard and
lyrics that sum things up
a little too well.

While the rest of the house rests, I'm
pirouetting and spinning in my bare feet
across the kitchen, eyes closed,
lost and present,
scattered and one,
all at the same time

70

Funeral Procession

I moved over to the left and
slowed down, as eight men
carried the casket down the sidewalk and
into the hearse

A hill of pink flowers adorned
the top, with eight
stern and silent faces along
the sides, an additional man
by the hearse's door to guide it in

I slowed down and drove by and
turned off my radio – the melody now
unwelcome noise, as I navigated
out of the neighborhood, going
perpendicular across one-way streets
to a destination that had lost its surety.

71

Time

Time will count down for you, so
don't

Don't do that to yourself; do not
count down the minutes, the days
Do not look forward to the
next good thing

The thing is now, there is no use
setting the timer
It's not worth waiting for the bell

The bell will ring.
The time will stop
(on its own)

There is no use doing its job on your dime

Getting Real

"I can get real," she says,
"These days
I don't have any family."

Her arms are crossed and
her vernacular is rough
but her eyes are tender and
sad and
carry the weight
of each person not in her life

73

Traffic

My poor anxious soul is a claustrophobic mess
I'm desperate
for open air. Windows down, open road,
outside, outside, outside

I ache for it the way
my lungs ache for air
And sometimes
that road
is the only place where I find breath

This small town has spoiled me rotten, I can
no longer handle
city driving – the open roads
of the country speak to my anxious heart
While the constant stop
and start of the city
only feeds it

74

Today

Today I will weed the garden
return emails
finally catch up on the laundry

Today I will make the bed when I wake up
and catch up on my lesson plans.
Read a little, wash the walls
tidy up the halls

Today I will move forward with
a productive eye
instead of the stagnant spot I sit
waiting for it all to pass me by

Wild Sky/If Nothing Else

If nothing else
I have the wild sky
from a winter's setting sun
And the softness the world takes
when under a sea of orange
and pink
and criss-cross clouds

The Past

My heart is stuck in the past, wedged
between a lovely lie and the
painful truth
– between a beautiful memory
and fear of what's to come

Waiting

I now have the cleanest
most organized purse
and my credit cards are all aligned

and my emails are all responded to
and my inbox is so neat
and I caught up on some reading,
too

I've walked to throw things out and to check the windows
countless times
counting footsteps, heartbeats, breaths

I've drained 70% of my phone
and 90% of my energy
because waiting is not an issue
but what I do while I wait is

78

Wake Up

I woke up just in time

to find myself knee deep
in decisions I made while I was asleep

79

While Heavy in Thought at a Stoplight

As I slow to a stop, one thousand
emotions pulling my face into
contorted shapes

a man pulls up
next to me, in the righthand lane
with the same weighed down look, the same
lines dug into his face, his eyes focused
down on his steering wheel, the same way
mine just were

At green, we go our ways
he turns right, I go left
he never sees me, but we both
acknowledge the traffic light's change
like a taking in of a stern reminder
from a person of authority

80

Triumph

And in the end, I didn't triumph
with any grand
finale, or
climactic scene

but rather

with the silent understanding
that I was here, that I
made it here, that
each small step, one foot
in front of the other
got me to
another day
one more step in front of the other

still breathing
still moving
still forward going

If Nothing Else (Pt 2)

If nothing else
I can leave this world knowing
I loved with reckless abandon
speaking in tongues only
the heart can decode, and
listening
to nothing more
than the songs of my soul

Extremes

The weather doesn't know what it wants today.

Blue skies, thunderstorms, sometimes
downpours
while the sun is shining, vacillating
wildly from one extreme
to the other.

Today is not a day
for middle grounds.

Dr. Katz

This little feline hops up and walks up
and down my lap, nuzzling my chin and leaning into
my hand. He purrs loudly as he circles, once, twice
sitting down,
paws kneading my leg, his wet nose
prodding at my wrist

"We call him Doctor Katz," she jokes, "because he does this
to our daughter
when she's sick or upset
or crying ."

I give a weak smile, a
gentle pat, shrugging away what I want to say:

"Not just your child, apparently."

Cycle of Broken

Two
broken people, from
broken families, broken
backgrounds, came together
just to break each other
more – and continue the pattern
of creating broken people
in broken backgrounds, going forth
on broken paths

Patching

Nothing
has helped patch
together my shattered
soul quite like
finding
pieces and parts
of my soul
in the people I meet

Fleeting

I dreamt of you last night,
vivid and consuming and
gone as I woke up
faded from memory before I had the chance
to collect and recollect

Even in my dreams you are ephemeral
and just outside of reach

87

Burn

When you have burned through a year
with worry
with stress
with waiting
with anxiety

it does not help to list off the things you've done
and accomplished, places you've been, and
tasks you have completed

It is counting the branches, the leaves
the rings on the trunk
of a tree in the midst of a forest fire

175

88

From the Mouth of a Yoga Teacher

Breathe in, breathe out
Be okay with your
emotions, your
thoughts
Yourself.

Let go.

Let go of tension in the neck, the shoulders,
the mind.
Be okay with where your thoughts take you.

Breathe in, breathe out
Let go of your attachments, your need for
specific outcomes
specific resolutions

Resolutions in general

Give yourself a chance to embrace
uncertainty
And the impermanence of everything.

Breathe in, breathe out
Breathe.
You're okay.

Be aware.
Be okay.
Do
Not
Judge

I am the yoga instructor I desperately need
for myself.

Jeans

He was like the perfect pair of jeans.

The kind that hug every line and curve
even the parts you feel are
out of proportion — the parts that make you feel
like you'd never truly be a proper fit, at any size.

And falling for him was
as effortless
as sliding those jeans on.

His Lover's Picture Beside His Desk

She's supposed to be looking
seductively into the camera, this
memento he has
to remember her by
throughout the day – instead,
her eyes are cold, her lips tight,
as she looks sternly into the camera
like she's about to yell at him a second time

A Few Words on Love

Perhaps
in the end
love
is not what blinds us
but
what binds us

92

Voices

Of all the voices
inside my head
the one that speaks only at
quiet, heavy times,
stating:
"You're going to be all right."

Is the one I try
to listen to
the most

93

Self

I do not need to find myself
I am myself

Whatever's been uncovered or discovered
whatever will change or remain
I ride alongside what makes this me
the person I was, is, and will be

I do not need to find myself
I am myself

I am not a thing to find
like a lucky penny or lost shoe
I am not an X on a map
or buried in the sand

I am events and evolutions, epiphanies
and stagnancies
meandering paths and sharp right turns
in every holding pattern and
express lane and
dead-end street

These that cannot be caught with a net or
tied to a rock
but gently unraveled with time

Something you can only take in
like a wild and frightening story, no
endings or finales
Just bookmarks and dog-eared cornered and
well-worn pages and fraying edges

I am exactly me when I'm not myself
I am still me, even when I do not want to be
It's still there, something to carry, regardless
of weight
when it's unbearably heavy or unbearably light

Whatever that me is destined to be, both
in and for this world.

That breath is me, that heartbeat's me
that sigh and smile and closing eyes

It's all me

I do not need to find myself.
I am myself.

Force

Hope is a powerful
(ly destructive)
force

This Town

This town is just small enough
that the store manager asks about your day
the cashier makes small talk
and you greet other patrons with a smile

Just small enough that
runners wave as they run past their neighbors
and neighbors learn each others' names

My big city heart swells
how perfect these little, constant actions are
how lovely, these constant little reminders that we are sur-
rounded
by people, with good souls and intentions
That every single day we act and interact
with people with stories to tell
and connections desperate to be made

Just enough to remind you
that you are not alone.

Yes, this town is just small enough.

Moving

She tells me she's moving to Cali

and that's when I notice I am
surrounded by people
with either iron anchors or
readied sails

And God help those who have both rigged.

Vices

I have my vices.

I drink too much coffee, sometimes
substituting it for proper food, sometimes
swinging by a coffee shop in between appointments, errands
lulls in the day

I play music at all times, sometimes
dancing, sometimes singing, always
substituting it for silence

I am hooked onto my phone, returning
emails and messages and texts and
keeping up with what my friends are doing
and checking sites and profiles and substituting
it for a moment
where I am actually alone with my thoughts.

I waste too much gasoline, driving around
everywhere, intentionally detouring, windows down,
music blaring, coffee in hand,
my phone tempting me from the passenger seat

Letting the wind whip my hair around as it
comes in from the sides, around my windshield,
dancing in circles inside my car, substituting it

for facing the wind
head on

98

Home

"There's no place
like home
for the holidays."

If only we knew
what home actually looked like.

"Home is where the heart is."

Ditto.

Calm Before the Storm

If this is her calm
before the storm

Then God help us
When the rain
actually starts
to fall

Cursory

I'm tired of cursory
I'm tired of the fleeting, superficial
move on to the next
8-second Vine, 2-line Tweet,
I'm exhausted and I need
more

As soon as I'm done
switching tabs and
checking my email

Puzzle

I am in a constant, desperate state
to see how my actions fit in
with the rest of the world.

As if my life, my actions
were a jigsaw piece
and – each day – I scan over the puzzle
to see
just where it fits
how it connects, how the angles of mine
line up, the divots and bumps
cut that way for a
proven reason

Every day, scanning a scattered product
with my little piece in hand
knowing that this misshapen collection
of cardboard and stock will help make
a gorgeous picture
of a waterfall or kittens
or a cityscape or meadow
a final image on a grand scale

102

To-Do

I got out of the habit of
to-do lists, of starting my day
with pen and pad
writing out what needs to be done

It's time to get back, to list out
the chores, the errands, the meetings,
the hopes and aspirations for the day

instead of winging it by the hour, accomplishing
a scattered, random fraction
of what I could, had I not set myself adrift

I need to get back to writing out
guidelines, parameters, things that make the day
worth it,
productive, using pen and pad
to steer me right.

Words

If I cradle your words
any more
than I already do, they'd take
physical form

nestled

in the palm of my hand

or

the crook of my elbow

tucked in by my torso
below the heart
warm and
protected

This Part of Town

"I'm desperately lonely," she seems to cry out from
her spot on the bus
with the look, the slouch, the
glances around,
as if broadcasting her sorrows to the world.

"We all are, hon," the rest of the bus sings back
with eyes on the floor, their phone, out the window

with people holding poles, handles, bags,
other people's hands.

105

Sleepwalker

I woke up to find myself sitting up in bed
and crying
large tears spilling
down my face, with reckless abandon
like a child after a nightmare
calling for their mom

I don't know how I got there, how it
came to pass
that I'd be sobbing in my sleep, upright
with my elbows on my knees
or how long I'd been there, or what
exactly woke me up

Even awake, I kept on crying
like a leak that refused to fix
remarking on how deep the cuts must run
if this is what happens when I dream

After the Storm

The trees are painted
white after the storm, snow
on every branch

This beautiful addition, this
scenic strain, putting them
at greater risk
of snapping in half

Waiting Game

In many ways, my life has been
a waiting game, waiting
for the weekend, the chance to quit
my job
Waiting for the movie to end, because I
can't sit still

Waiting to hear from a friend again, waiting
for a vacation, for reprieve, waiting
for resolution, waiting for a
crossroads to force a conclusion on me

Waiting to the point that it exhausts me
and I am without energy, without ability
for whatever it was I was waiting for

In many ways, my life has been a waiting game
And the only way to win is to breathe in
breathe out
and temporarily stave off the weight of the future

108

Blinded

Optimism: to simultaneously be
driven and
blinded
by hope

But

I guess, there are
worse things
to be blinded by
then something so
deceivingly lovely

109

Cutting Through Vermont

At the base of the
mountain range, the one with
snowcapped peaks and summits disappearing
into the clouds, the kind of vista that
grabs you from miles away and
stretches out beyond your scope, making you
believe in heavens and gods and
forces higher than ourselves

stood a trailer park 3 rows long,
rusted roofs covering
dilapidating walls
run down plastic playground toys
litter the yard, its
single paved road running
parallel with my own

Shades Drawn

With the shades drawn, I am convinced
the skies are grey,
only to peak out
and see
a gentle dawn upon me

A Walk

I need a walk

a long walk, one that
winds its way through forests and lakes
One where the autumn leaves fly from the trees
and float, like
confetti across my way

I need to walk
to walk a long walk, one that
can clear my mind, one where moving
legs and arms and feet prove
that this feeling does not actually
paralyze

I need
open air to remind me I'm not actually suffocating
And a sun shining down as proof that
the sky isn't falling

I need a walk, a long, long walk
one where I don't return until I have the answers I need

Slip

"Are you around?" she asks, and I type back:
"I'm afraid.

Around!

Around!
I meant around."

"Freudian slip?"
she asks.

(I laugh and agree and ask what she wants)

All the while refraining from replying back

"More than you know."

Unrequited

I spoke so many words
to the empty air in front of me
imagining you were here in its
place to hear them

Instead, the vacuum of your absence
swirled
in the gap between what I
needed and what I had,

creating a hurricane in lieu of being
heard, letting me know
just how much this desire could destroy

114

Doors

Of all the things to be haunted by, I'm haunted by doors.

Images, memories,
real-life glimpses of these doors.

Doors I'd walk up to, through, with desperate hopes
of seeing him again.
Doors I'd walk through in hopes
he'd walk through as well.
Doors that would be
shut and
latched and
beautiful and delicate time would be allowed to pass.

Doors that do nothing to hold in memories, to
hold back emotions, to cordon off a single feeling
into four straight,
narrow,
predictable walls.

115

Taking My Life Back

Sometimes
"Take back my life" feels like a daily task
like each morning I must wrangle it
as I prepare coffee, as I put on my shoes

And as I write an email, pausing to walk
down the hall, retrieving my life
from whatever has it now,
prying the fingers of what has it in its grasp

Finishing tasks, the hours, the obstacles
all the while playing a twisted game of catch
where an outside force snatches and I must get it back

Sometimes
when asked about my day, I want to say:
"On top of all those things, I took my life back eight whole
times
knowing full well something will take it again – almost like
I have no control of its whereabouts.
No control over what takes it away."

Saving Grace

I'm not his saving grace
so much
a pebble in his shoe

And there's nothing
that can change that
no matter what I do.

The Words I Didn't Say

There's a lull
at the end
of our phone call

and I keep silent.

even though
three words are
bubbling
at the base of my throat

Words that are
dying
to come out. Words that
have been there for
way longer
than I had previously
thought.

But,

I smile

into the receiver instead, all at once
elated and

frightened
when I discover

just how much I meant the words I didn't say

118

The Production and the Dance

Did you know

When I dance, the past
and
the future
have no choice but to sit
on the sidelines
like
a faithful audience

their hands on their laps, silence on their lips
as I attempt a pirouette, a leg lift

When I dance, the floor
and
anxiety and
uncertainty
are reduced to stagehands, fretting
over lights and music, scurrying around
dressed in all black to remain
unseen

When I dance, the only
vibrations
and
energy

I feel is
the thumping bass, the melody,
the sound of feet against the floor

So loud it rings in my ears and I smile
right up until the curtain falls

119

Branded

It's the mark
of a fool

But there's no other brand
I'd rather be scarred with

120

Bright Yellow Car

Her car is compact and yellow and in the
righthand lane
I drive past and, inside, she's hysterical, with
bright red face and mouth agape
a fist to her teeth as her whole body shakes

I try not to stare – her car
is her sanctuary, and God knows
I understand

And, because of that, I am desperate
to pull over, to get into
the passenger seat
and give her a hug in her sunny bright car
as she drives down this street I know too well

Mighty Tired Poetry

I'm getting mighty tired of my poetry
coming forth only
in times of great anguish
and anxiety

Like the only way to find beauty
is to first suffer
and the only way to survive suffering
is to find beauty

Concord

How I love this city

A place that snuck up on me during
road trips and detours
Like a planet in orbit circling back, time and again
until – before I knew it – it captured my heart.

How I adore this little city,
with its changing neighborhoods, its
light and dark paths – how I love
every park, every pothole,
every building and monument
every fresh coat of paint and every
ding and dent and scratch

I am drawn to this city, drawn to what I know and
what I don't yet know.
I'm drawn to the faces of those I pass by, drawn to
the smiles and pursed lips,
closed eyes, averted gazes
crossed arms and rogue grins

I am drawn to its history, its past and present and
future
I walk the streets, the familiar and the new and the
slightly terrifying

Desperate for more of its story, what makes it tick, and how
the rest of this story will unfold.

I am fond of the city

fond in a way I can't define, fond in a way
that is different and
undeniable

I am an expat from another place, finding
solace in how the sun grazes over the treetops, how
the stars fill its sky
and how the street lamps illuminate
passages I've never been down before.

Burning Woman

Today is a burning up kind of day

The kind that starts in the pit of your heart
and sets the rest on fire

And I do my best not to run, but to let
the fire burn, for as long and as bright
as it needs.

Burn until there's nothing
but ashes
for me to scatter as I walk into the wind

Spirit

I was a wild spirit who thrived
on the fuck yeahs and definitelys
but stopped dead in her tracks, convincing
herself it all would eventually
kill her

So I laid on level ground,
settling in and rooting down,
using the solid earth to plant my feet
and stand and be strong enough to see
that the reasonable rationality
would eventually kill me
too, at a slower
but guaranteed pace

125

Passion

I am simultaneously spurned on
and burned alive by passion.

No one warns you that
a fevered excitement for life

might result in night sweats
and delirium

126

Merrimack River

The Merrimack continues to churn, leaving
thin layers of ice
on the rocks it hits

A vibrant, violent blue,
a reminder of
the key vital need
in moving forward
with force.

Airplanes

I exhausted myself
writing love letters like
paper airplanes into
the sky

Now I dance with my
fingers through the air
as my shoulders tire out
and I face the wind
head-on

128

Black Spot

Don't let that black spot
in your life shift
to the forefront of your corneas

blocking out
the rising sun, the way
the beams hit the grass

Or move to the
base of your throat
blocking that
first breath on
a brisk morning

or your ears, making it
impossible to hear what it is
you need to hear

Let the black spot be
where and
what it needs to be

A pixel on a canvas
a dot alongside a full prism
of colors
and sensations

Red Sky at Night

The sun sets easy
over the mountains: Red sky at night.
Sailor's delight.
Storm has passed.

Two minutes later I drive
into rain, orange skies still present
in the rear view mirror.

Walden

She quotes Walden, saying that
people's lives are a
quiet desperation

She says it not as an indictment or
a call to arms, but as fact, as
inarguable fact, as if stripped away
of the option of choice, speaking of it
the way a prisoner speaks of his shackles

And she says these words with a quiet force
and sad eyes, she says these words
a few times more
as if trying to give the last shards of her spirit
the swan song it deserves

Scent

How much can a smell weigh?
Darling, you tell me.

If I had to guess, I'd say it weighs
exactly as much as the heart can carry
as I walk down the hall
smelling scents that bring me back
to fragile, cherished times.

Advice for Writers

Allow yourself to be bad

Allow yourself to be the shittiest little writer
you have ever come across
Allow yourself to sound like a clunky, clumsy
adolescent version of yourself

Give yourself permission to suck

Give yourself permission to make
complete and total nonsense and
garbage, permission to be knee-deep
in the muck of your own ramblings

And maybe, perhaps
while you're in the midst
of creating garbage and muck
you find you've made gems
far more often than you'd think

Bankrupt

Watch me
as I go bankrupt – all the while
saying:
"I guess
this is the price
of admission."

Breathe

I have this breath.

I have this inhale and this exhale.

Nothing more.

And someday I won't have even that.

I have this breath, this
simple breath, and
that is it.

I do not have the future
I do not have the past
I do not have control

I just have this breath.

I do not have the outcomes
I do not have the answers
or even ownership of
the questions themselves

I do not own the racing thoughts in my head
or the ache in my chest
or the body that surrounds them
or the soul that transcends them

I cannot claim health or illness, staking it
like territory

I cannot own loved ones, or their actions, or
the forces of the world
I can't own grudges or regrets

I own nothing presented by fear and anxiety
I do not own the uncertainty, the doubt
or the concept of stress itself

I do not have a crystal ball or a time machine
or a way to read thoughts, predict all outcomes
manipulate the world
I do not have any of that

Just this inhale.
Just this exhale.
Not the one before it.
Not the one after it.

I do not have how things evolve and change, or
what will come, go, stay, remain
I do not have what will be lost, found, discarded
discovered or ignored

I do not have anything
or anything else
but this inhale,
this exhale.

At the end of the day, stripping down

what I foolishly call or want to call my own
Stripping away the things and thoughts I cling to

This is what I have.

I have this breath
and someday I won't have that

This breath, this inhale, as cherished and
as fragile
as the things I worry about
as the memories, the plans that go awry
all the people, the events, the things
I will meet, I will miss, I will miss out on
Everything I will love and lose
going forth like the exhale from my lungs

So I will breathe in, and I will breathe out

This simple breath, this
reminder of what matters
This reminder of what is

.

135

Ownership

I will hold this sadness close
like the sweetest thing, cup it with both
hands, let it swirl in my palms
until it settles down

I won't attempt to stop it, or
tamp it down, throw it out, or deny
it's here. I will pirouette with it
across the room, my delicate little
dancing partner as
tears stream down my face

The Mountains

The mountains
do not
make my problems seem
small

But they do
make my soul
feel large

Dorian Gray

I warned her that her lover is
the Picture of Dorian Gray
but
in reverse.

Instead of the portrait taking in
the ugliness
and sin
so he can be and
do
whatever he wants

Instead

he lets himself be ugly
so the image can stay
pristine

138

Vulnerable

Let me lay bare my soul
to show you're not alone
in this naked rawness

Pressure Valve

Please do not see the
constant gift of love, expecting
nothing in return, as some sort of
selfless act

It is simply pressure valve
relief
for what builds up in me
every second of every day
to the point that I might burst
otherwise

During My Walk

I whispered what I needed to say
to the pines and birches, bemoaning
my troubles, what can't be said
in hallways
on a narrow path

I let out what my heart was aching for
to the canopies of the trees, waiting
on the wind to carry what
I said away
to let this pain fall
behind on the trail
as I walked past

Instead I found it
followed me home, retracing its steps until
it was back inside, and as I was
removing my shoes, it created a spot
for itself on my couch, looking
over at me expectantly

141

What Happens

If you fall in love with anything
but the soul
If you fall for actions and gestures, or
looks and charm, if you become attached
because of circumstance or ease, if you fall
for the details, the surface level things

What happens
when those details are taken away?

Emotional Hangover

These days
I walk around
emotionally hungover,
when I used to be simply
drunk on life.

Noise

I'm getting used to the silence, getting used
to talking walks and
washing dishes in peace, without
a song or idle chatter
to fill the space.

I'm getting used to driving
in silence, running errands
and running laps as so, doing things
in the deafening and
overwhelming
quiet.

I'm getting used to turning off
the buzz and the busy-ness, the
white noise, and welcoming
the powerful backdrop
of the
actual noise
around me.

144

Continuum

Darling,
what if

We had known each other in another life

and

The love was so
profound, that it rippled out
across time and space, affecting
the lifetimes that followed.

Darling,
what if

Everything
in this life
was disrupted, purely so
we could meet and
fall in love
again.

The consequence of those ripples
extending
into the present day

ABBY ROSMARIN

Echoes from something
much larger

back when space and time were on our side.

145

Indecision

The rolling mists of New Hampshire
travel like nomads through the valley, just after
the temperature dipped and soared

This flux in weather turns the land
into a panoramic shot, this constant change
makes the world surreal

It is the prettiest consequence
of indecision
that you will ever see

146

Okay

How much work
it takes
to say,
"I'm not okay."

Like the phonemes and
apostrophes
get clogged between our teeth

Like muscle memory
prevents
anything less
than a smile

147

On the Drive Back Home from Heartache

On the drive back home
from heartache, the kind
that leaves one in
tears by the steering wheel

the traffic slowed and stopped before
going again
in the distance were flashing blue
and white and red lights, two cops
directing traffic, single file towards
the other side of the road, while my side is
a festival of lights

The officers direct
us around two cars, or what remains
of two after a head-on
collision. The lights and glass
in shatters, hoods
crushed, the engines smoking

Two police cars, a fire truck, one
ambulance, no passengers in sight

Through my blurry eyes, the lights are a mosaic

of emergency and brake lights,
street lamps and street flares
and a semi full moon supervising it all

No One Reads Poetry

No one reads poetry
and those who do still don't

Those that do digest and
pause, get in and
simmer

They experience a few words and
a couple lines like
something to be carried

And they do
carry and
digest, simmer and
experience

But
really
no one reads poetry
anyway

That's When You Know

When the memories fade
and lose their zing, when the
edges sand down with time,
when the people, places, and things
remind only in whispers and
echoes, when the old photos become trite and
mementos useless

When every earthly thing
takes a step into the background, when
the surface level, for all its depths,
is stripped away
and you realize that they were all just
trimmings
bells and whistles for the soul at the
heart of it all, a soul you miss
in ways only your own soul
can say, in ways that transcend every
earthly thing
When you realize what haunts you are not memories
but the essence of the person themselves

That's when you know you're fucked

Pass On

How desperate we are
to pass on
before we pass on

Our story, our knowledge
our lessons,
our genes

Passing on before
we pass on

Timeline

When you realize you were never meant
to know, that you were never
given the timeline of events
in advance, never handed
the blueprints of the future – no matter
how much you tried, no matter how much
the uncertainty ate at you – because you needed
each moment
to reveal in order, for the future
to arrive in piecemeal form, you needed
daily and tiny
installments in order to process
the plans, the blueprints, the changes – to properly digest
what awaited you
in time

Foreboding

It was the lingering smile after
a simple joke, a lingering feeling
that signaled just how much
I was getting in over my head

And if I had to do it all over again – knowing
full well what awaited me below the surface
I would, without hesitation,
dive right back into the deep end

Continuing

I will eat oatmeal in the morning again.

And I will eat apples as snacks and
mop once a week; I'll throw my
clothes in the hamper and
return emails again.

I'll plan meals and carry out chores.
Run errands and clean.
I will put groceries away and
clean the litter box.
I'll stay hydrated and go to bed early
and research schools in the morning.

All the little things that fall apart
when everything else feels like it's been
flipped on its head.

Grateful

I'm grateful for
a short and
gentle winter, reminding me
spring renewal does not always
have to come
after suffering a frozen death

Trails

I was never meant
to follow the footsteps
of my mom, but to
muddy my knees, blazing
a new trail
of my own

156

Strength

I carry you.

I carry you with me as
I go about my life. As I open
car doors and unlock windows
and stop at stop signs. I carry you
with me as I talk with colleagues
and send emails and
go about chores.

I carry you with me in every joke,
every comment, every sigh,
in every interaction and thought and
consideration. I carry you with me
through every dream and daydream, through
every fit of inspiration, every
pause for reflection, through
whatever twists and turns I find.

I carry you with me even as
the weight of it all rests on my shoulders
and my muscles and bones and
heart aches.

I carry you as I carry on with life.

And then there are moments
when I swear you are next to me
— next to and
with me, beside and a part of me

And the subtle strength from it carries me
for as long as the feeling lasts

Beautiful World

How beautiful
the world became, once I started
seeing every interaction like a dance
between souls

Tell me, stranger,
how shall we dance today?

Catching Feelings

Let me "catch feelings"
until my palms are blistered
and my shoulders are sore
– for what good are soft hands
on a weak, calloused soul

Life Path

The path might be messy,

but

I'd rather go to the grave all
muddied up
than as a pristine,
inauthentic replica of
who I thought I had to be.

About the Author

Abby Rosmarin is a lot of things, including someone who writes about herself in the third person. Abby is the author of *I'm Just Here for the Free Scrutiny* as well as *Chick Lit & Other Formulas for Life*. When not writing, Abby is a registered yoga teacher, a commercial model, and desperately on the run from being a real adult. You can catch her shenanigans on Twitter & Instagram (both @thatabbyrose) or on her blog at thatabbyrose.wordpress.com.

Thought Catalog, it's a website.

www.thoughtcatalog.com

Social

facebook.com/thoughtcatalog

twitter.com/thoughtcatalog

tumblr.com/thoughtcatalog

instagram.com/thoughtcatalog

Corporate

www.thought.is

www.ingramcontent.com/pod-product-compliance
Lightning Source LLC
LaVergne TN
LVHW041314080426
835513LV00008B/451